ALMA DE GROEN was born in New Zealand in 1941. In 1964 she settled in Australia where, under the influence of the new theatre movement, she began writing plays in 1968. Between 1969 and 1972 she spent four years overseas among artists in England, France and Canada; and while in Canada in 1970 won a national playwriting competition with her short work, *The Joss Adams Show*. This received a workshop performance by the Shakespearean Festival Theatre, Stratford, Ontario, and a season at the Studio Laboratory Theatre, Toronto. Since then it has been performed in most Australian capital cities and in London and New Zealand.

Her first play, *The Sweatproof Boy*(later shortened into *Perfectly All Right*) was presented at the Nimrod Street Theatre in 1972; on her return to Australia *The After-Life of Arthur Cravan* was selected by the first Australian National Playwrights Conference(1973) and had a season the same year at the Jane Street Theatre, Sydney. This was followed by *Going Home*(1976) and *Chidley*(1977) both of which had their première seasons in Melbourne. In 1980 *Going Home* was broadcast on ABCTV as part of the Australian Theatre Festival II. *Vocations* received a workshop at the 1981 Australian National Playwrights Conference and its première in Melbourne in 1982. Alma De Groen was awarded the 1985 AWGIE award for her television adaptation of *Man of Letters*, and has written scripts for the television series *Singles* and *Rafferty's Rules*. *The Rivers of China* was workshopped at the 1986 National Playwrights Conference and had its première in Sydney in 1987.

ELIZABETH PERKINS is Associate Professor of English at James Cook University of North Queensland.

THE RIVERS OF CHINA

by

Alma De Groen

CURRENCY PRESS • SYDNEY

CURRENCY PLAYS
General Editor: Katharine Brisbane

First published in 1988 by
Currency Press Pty Ltd,
P.O. Box 452, Paddington, NSW 2021 Australia.

National Library of Australia
Cataloguing-in-Publication data
De Groen, Alma, 1941-
    The Rivers of China.

    ISBN 0 86819 171 X

    1. Mansfield, Katherine, 1888-1923, in fiction, drama, poetry,
    etc. 2.Gurdjieff, G.I. (Georges Ivanovitch), 1872-1949.
    Drama. I. Title.

A822'.3

Typeset by Allette Systems P/L, Sydney.

Creative writing program assisted by the
Australia Council, the Federal Government's
arts funding and advisory body.

The Soul has Bandaged moments -
When too appalled to stir -
She feels some ghastly Fright come up
And stop to look at her

Salute her - with long fingers -
Caress her freezing hair -
Sip, Goblin, from the very lips
The Lover - hovered - o'er -
Unworthy, that a thought so mean
Accost a Theme - so - fair -

The soul has moments of Escape -
When bursting all the doors -
She dances like a Bomb, abroad,
And swings upon the Hours...

The Soul's retaken moments -
When, Felon led along,
With shackles on the plumed feet,
And staples in the Song,

The Horror welcomes her, again,
These, are not brayed of Tongue -

Emily Dickinson

Contents

*Helen Morse as Katherine Mansfield in the Sydney Theatre
Company production. Photo : Hugh Hamilton*

Introduction

Elizabeth Perkins

Two plots interweave in *The Rivers of China*, the Fontainebleau narrative and the Sydney narrative, both involved with the life and death of the New Zealand-born writer Katherine Mansfield, and both concerned with the place of women and artists in a patriarchal society. The play is a natural development from Alma De Groen's six earlier stage plays, all of which are in some way concerned with women or artists, and sometimes with both, and which use the dramatic form of their action as part of their dramatic statement.

Gifted, sensitive and ardent, Kathleen Mansfield Beauchamp was born in 1888, the daughter of a prosperous Wellington merchant. Although children appear often in her work, and are treated with understanding, she grew up with a sense of purpose that went beyond home, husband and family. A generous need to love and be loved led her into chaotic and sometimes lasting relationships with men and women. She was disinherited by her mother, who disapproved of her relationships with women, suffered several miscarriages and perhaps an abortion, which made it impossible for her later to have children, contracted gonorrhea, which was not diagnosed for many years and gave her painful 'arthritis', and possibly even contracted tuberculosis from a small boy whom she temporarily adopted after the loss of her first child.

When the play opens, we seem to be a long way from Katherine Mansfield and her death from tuberculosis on the 9th January 1923 at the Gurdjieff Institute for the Harmonious Development of Man at Fontainebleau in France. The Sydney Hospital in which Audra works as a doctor and her friend Wayne as an orderly, is, like the Gurdjieff Institute, a place of healing. Although the time is the present, the patriarchal society we know has been replaced by a female dystopia in which inequalities are merely reversed;

women hold the power, and the writing of men is suppressed. Yet the poem of Emily Dickinson that Wayne quotes, expresses for him, as a second-class citizen, the same truth about the bandaged and shackled state of the soul as, in the real world, it has expressed for women over the last century. In the next hospital scene, the image of the bandaged soul is made visible, as Wayne mops around a bed on which lies the bandaged form of a young man who, like many of his sex, has apparently attempted suicide under the present regime.

Before this, however, the second narrative begins with Katherine entering the Gurdjieff Institute where she spends the last eight weeks of her life. This is followed by a chronologically earlier scene in which she tells her husband, the critic John Middleton Murry, of her intention to go to Fontainebleau rather than take a cottage in Cornwall, with the tempestuous D.H. Lawrence and Frieda as neighbours. Katherine's journey to seek physical and spiritual help from the Russian mystic is associated with a wish once made by her mother, that instead of marrying she had gone exploring 'the rivers of China'. The form of the play, in which unconventional sequences and juxtapositions are deliberately plotted, images the journey that a woman takes alone through territory that she is traditionally expected to traverse only with a man as guide.

These first five scenes, interweaving the narratives, reversing traditional roles, multiplying varied and unexpected relationships and transposing chronological time sequences, establish the shape and movement the play will take. They end with Katherine telling Gurdjieff, 'I believe you can do what I've dreamed might be done - cure my soul.'

The Fontainebleau narrative shows that Gurdjieff's programme of diet, dance and instruction extends Katherine's life long enough for her to develop some sense of the integrated 'I' she is seeking. At the end, however, she learns that in Gurdjieff's philosophy a woman has no soul, that she must have a man to help her evolve, and that it is wrong for a woman to aspire in life or in art. Gurdjieff holds the map, and no woman should attempt to explore alone the rivers of China. No records of conversation between Mansfield and

Gurdjieff exist, but Alma De Groen's play, making free use of Mansfield's journals and letters and the writing of Gurdjieff's disciples, dramatizes the underlying truth of Mansfield's encounter with Gurdjieff.

The female dystopia narrative, set in Sydney, avoids the Science Fiction mode by taking place not in the future, but in the present. Late in the play, with deliberately disorientating effect, Wayne and The Man see on video a ritual enactment of the genesis of the dystopia, when women evolved a superior mental power, the Medusa Look, to counteract the superior physical strength that for centuries assisted male dominance.

In the Sydney narrative, the artist figure is Rahel, a plastic surgeon who reconstructs The Man's face, and, assisting the healing process by the forbidden use of hypnosis, recreates in his mind the spirit of Katherine Mansfield who died some sixty years earlier. Rahel tells Wayne that she wanted to create 'a man who could be an equal, without being a danger', but she also does what patriarchal histories have done to the lives of women. As Rahel says, 'You can give anybody a history that never happened and they'll believe it.' Rahel's experiment gets out of control. The Man knows more than she gave him, and he inherits Katherine's disease as well as her indomitable creative spirit. Rahel offers to save The Man's life by restoring his former male spirit, but Wayne chooses to let the Man-Woman die, rather than lose the female spirit he has grown to love. In the context of Mansfield's life, Wayne's decision to let The Man die, reflects Murry's response to her last years of illness, when he seemed to have a half-conscious wish that she would die soon, leaving him in the appealing role of the bereaved lover of a stricken genius. The twelve years of their relationship and their marriage in 1918 probably meant more to both writers than an outsider can appreciate. After Mansfield's death, however, she was canonized in Murry's writing, and he promoted her image in a way that denied her status as a real woman, and for a time threatened her reputation as a serious writer.

As the act of an artist, Rahel's experiment raises questions about the relationship between form and spirit: a problem to which Mansfield gave a startlingly new emphasis in her stories, and one that Alma De Groen has addressed in her plays. The fate of The Man who is also Katherine Mansfield, opens complex questions that cannot be explained in terms of simple dichotomies of male and female, and body and spirit. Although Katherine Mansfield was very conscious of herself as a woman, in her life she often exchanged the traditional forms of male and female behaviour. At nineteen, she wrote that in her passion for another young woman, she felt 'more than half man', and she was emotionally and financially the supportive partner in her relationship with Murry. She relied often on the organising skill of her devoted friend Ida Baker, yet when tuberculosis was diagnosed in 1917, she was horrified to think that illness might force on her a traditional womanly dependence.

In Katherine Mansfield's writing, the ethical and aesthetic importance she gave to the use of form was inseparable from her life as a woman and as an artist: the ability to exchange forms of behaviour seems to be part of an acute awareness of the metaphysical concept of form and of the need to make that concept as expansive as possible. The structure of The Rivers of China also reproduces this expansive concept of form.

Katherine Mansfield was bored by the Suffragette meeting she attended in London in 1908, and left with the conviction that she would remedy such problems more effectively through her writing. Her idea of form was central to her ethical and political purpose - although she did not think of her work as political - but at the end of her life she still judged her achievement by patriarchal standards of form.

In 1912, the editor A.R. Orage, made a covert attack on Mansfield's work:

> The word virtue, like some others that belong to men, has been vulgarised by women's misappropriation: but its true meaning is still preserved from all botchers and sensation-seekers. The young artist who is virtuous will live for his art so that it may rank with the excellent. He will practise the duties of artists, cutting himself off from distracting influences, building up his power by practising in large and severe forms, fortifying his resolution by familiarity with the lives and works of great men. He will thus en-

sure the permanent health of his own work by cultivat-
ing his own character.

We see this now as male dominated art barricading itself
behind large and severe forms when it recognizes a real
threat from female genius. Mansfield's intricate short
stories are belittled and rendered insignificant and harm-
less. Yet her honesty as an artist allowed her to see that
there was some helpful truth in Orage's criticism, and it
was in pursuit of 'the permanent health of [her] own work'
that she took herself to Gurdjieff. Nine years after Orage
wrote this criticism, she sent him a letter thanking him 'for
everything': Orage, she said, taught her to write and to
think, and showed her what was to be done and what not
to do. It happened, too, that in 1922 it was Orage who in-
troduced her to Gurdjieff's work. At Fontainebleau,
Mansfield met Olga Ivanovna, who later married the ar-
chitect Frank Lloyd Wright, and who reported a conversation in which Mansfield admitted that she had written no
tragedies, novels or romances:

Later she told me she felt so wretched at that moment she
would have given anything if she could have answered
at least one 'yes' to the 'big' things.

In *The Rivers of China*, even Rahel's experiment with a
female spirit in a male body is part of a concern with evolv-
ing new ideas about form that would eventually make it impossible for any artist to experience Mansfield's distress
because she had not used any of the 'big' forms in her work.

Rahel enacts the visionary, challenging role of art that
Mansfield's stories also perform, many of which quietly
subvert attitudes towards women and their acceptance of
the limitations society imposes on them. A vision of true
equality of sex and gender allows Rahel to see beyond the
fear that makes the dominant women simply reverse the old
hierarchies. Her subversive graffiti, inspirational quota-
tions from male poets like Keats and Browning, also in-
voke other artists, like the poet Homer and the painter
Andrea del Sarto. The lines from 'Andrea del Sarto', which
are an important signifier on stage during the first act are,
however, doubly ironic. The masculinist language again
seems to exclude female aspiration, and when the lines are
put back into their context in Browning's poem, we find

that the artist admits that his reach does *not* exceed his grasp, and he suggests that his wife Lucrezia is partly responsible for his failure.

'My Lord Fool', which replaces Browning's line at the beginning of the second act, is a different kind of signifier. This is not part of Rahel's graffiti, but one of the subversive signifiers of the play itself, and of Katherine Mansfield's life. In *Henry IV Part One* the phrase is spoken by a man, and its Shakespearian context is relevant only because Hotspur also is a rebel. According to Murry, Mansfield wanted the quotation as an epigraph to the collection *Bliss and Other Stories*, and it was also used as an epigraph to the enigmatic story 'This Flower', which she wrote in 1919. Murry had the full quotation inscribed on Mansfield's tombstone, as 'words which had long been cherished by her and were to prove prophetic':

> But I tell you, my lord fool, out of this nettle danger, we pluck this flower, safety.

What the phrase 'My Lord Fool' signifies in *The Rivers of China* is more complex than Murry might have understood. It suggests irony and compassion, important qualities in Mansfield's writing. It also contributes to the questioning of the relationship between male and female that is part of the play's context, and that places Katherine Mansfield and her work at the heart of the action.

Townsville, 1987

References

Alpers, Anthony. *The Life of Katherine Mansfield* (London: Jonathan Cape, 1980)

De Groen, Alma. Interview in *LiNQ*, Vol.14, No.3, 1986.

Fullbrook, Kate. *Katherine Mansfield* (Brighton: Harvester Press, 1986)

Keller, Bruce. '*Exploring The Rivers of China,*' *New Theatre: Australia* (December 1987)

Mansfield, Katherine. *Collected Stories of Katherine Mansfield* (London: Constable, 1945)

Moore, James. *Gurdjieff and Mansfield* (London: Routledge & Kegan Paul, 1980)

Nott, C.S. *Teachings of Gurdjieff: The Journal of a Pupil* (London: Routledge & Kegan Paul, 1961)

O'Sullivan, Vincent and Scott, Margaret eds. *The Collected Letters of Katherine Mansfield* 2 vols. (Oxford: Clarendon Press, 1984)

Ouspensky, P.D. *In search of the Miraculous: Fragments of An Unknown Teaching* (London: Routledge & Kegan Paul, 1950)

The Fourth Way: A Record of Talks and Answers to Questions based on the teachings of G.I.Gurdjieff (London: Routledge & Kegan Paul, 1957)

Perkins, Elizabeth. 'Form and Transformation in the plays of Alma De Groen,' *Australasian Drama Studies* (October 1987)

Peters, Fritz. *Boyhood with Gurdjieff* (London: Gollancz, 1964. rpt. Santa Barbara: Capra Press, 1980)

Stead,C.K.ed. *The Letters and Journals of Katherine Mansfield* (London: Constable, 1945)

Frank Gallacher as Gurdjieff in the Sydney Theatre Company production. Photo: Hugh Hamilton.

Above: Patrick Dickson as John Middleton Murry and Helen
Morse as Katherine Mansfield. Below: John Howard as The
Man and Linden Wilkenson as Rachel. Sydney Theatre Company
production. Photos: Hugh Hamilton.

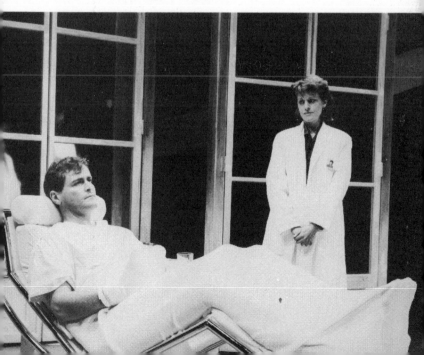

Above: Marcus Graham as Wayne and John Howard as The Man. Below: Patrick Dickson as Asanov, Linden Wilkinson as Lidia, Jenny Vuletic as Vera and Helen Morse as Katherine Mansfield. Sydney Theatre Company production. Photos: Hugh Hamilton.

THE RIVERS OF CHINA was workshopped at the 1986 Australian National Playwrights' Conference, directed by Peter Kingston and was first performed by the Sydney Theatre Company at the Wharf Theatre on 9 September 1987 with the following cast:

KATHERINE MANSFIELD	Helen Morse
WAYNE SHUTE	Marcus Graham
THE MAN	John Howard
GEORGEI IVANOVITCH GURDJIEFF/MATTHEW	Frank Gallacher
JOHN MIDDLETON MURRY/ MARK/ASANOV	Patrick Dickson
AUDRA/GIRL/VERA	Jenny Vuletic
RAHEL/LIDIA	Linden Wilkinson

Directed by Peter Kingston
Designed by Eamon D'Arcy

Music suggested for Act Two, Scene Two is *Journey to Inaccessible Places* by Gurdjieff and Thomas de Hartmann performed by Herbert Henck and Trilok Gurtu on Wergo SM 1035-6.

CHARACTERS

KATHERINE MANSFIELD, thirty-four
WAYNE SHUTE, late teens, early twenties
THE MAN, early thirties
GEORGEI IVANOVITCH GURDJIEFF/MATTHEW, mid to late
   forties
JOHN MIDDLETON MURRY/MARK/ASANOV, thirty-three
AUDRA/GIRL/VERA, late twenties
RAHEL/LIDIA, thirties or forties

SETTING

Gurdjieff's Institute for the Harmonious Development of Man
at Fontainebleau in the nineteen twenties, and a Sydney Hospital
in the present.

ACT ONE

SCENE ONE

WAYNE'*s room. The lights come up on* WAYNE *and* AUDRA *in bed.*

WAYNE: ... The soul has moments of Escape -
When bursting all the doors -
She dances like a Bomb, abroad,
And swings upon the Hours. . .

The Soul's retaken moments -
When, Felon led along,
With shackles on the plumed feet,
And staples in the Song,

The Horror welcomes her, again. . .

When I recite Emily Dickinson, I *am* Emily Dickinson.
    [AUDRA *gets up.*]
Audra?

AUDRA: I'm on call.
    [*She starts to dress.*]

WAYNE: I don't believe it! I made dinner. I thought you'd stay over.
    [*Pause.*]
When am I going to see you?

AUDRA: You'll see me at the hospital.

WAYNE: You know what I mean. I mean when am I going to see you?

AUDRA: I'll let you know.

WAYNE: Was it the poetry?

AUDRA: I'm a doctor, Wayne. I don't have time for words.

WAYNE: You're seeing someone else.

AUDRA: I'm not seeing anyone. We have our own lives to lead.

WAYNE: Speak for yourself.
    [AUDRA *picks up her bag. She crosses to* WAYNE.]

AUDRA: Look, Wayne: you're cute, you're funny, you make me laugh - and when I can get you to shut up, I enjoy going to bed with you. That's all there is to it. You either accept things as they are, or not at all. I'll see you on the ward.

[AUDRA *exits. He waits a safe interval.*]

WAYNE: [*shouting*] *Bitch!* Rotten bitch! I hate you. I hate all women! I wish you'd disappear off the face of the earth.

[*He flings himself back on the pillows, feels around underneath and pulls out a packet of lollies. He munches disconsolately.*]

Bitch.

[*He turns on the radio.*]

FEMALE ANNOUNCER: . . . Baffled by an incident involving a man who is reported to have fallen from the top of the A.M.P. Building at Circular Quay shortly before midday. Startled office workers reported seeing the figure as it plummeted to the street below, but surprisingly, no trace of a body has been found. An extensive search of the area failed to account for the disappearance of the man, whose fall was witnessed by upwards of forty people . . . Suicides by young men in New South Wales have risen in 1987* to -

[WAYNE *switches it off.*]

WAYNE: I've never told Audra I want to be a writer. I quote other people's poetry and slip in one of mine alongside Stevie Smith or whoever:

> Words which have never been born
> Or seen the light
> Shimmering on the edge of Mind
> Perilous ghosts . . .

[*He stops, considering, then starts to exit.*]

> 'Falling without sound . . .' [*Approvingly*]
> 'Dying on the haunted air . . .'

[*He exits.*]

---

*   [or the year in which the play is presented.]

SCENE TWO

Fontainebleau 1922. The gallery above the cowshed.
KATHERINE *and* GURDJIEFF *enter. There are faint sounds of
bicycle bells and distant shouts and laughter.* GURDJIEFF
studies KATHERINE *through a haze of cigarette smoke.*

KATHERINE: Well. It all sounds wonderfully good and simple
and what one needs. . .Perhaps I might go and unpack . . .?
[GURDJIEFF *continues his silent regard.* KATHERINE
moves to the window using her stick.]
What are they doing over there?
GURDJIEFF: They dig foundation for Turkish bath.
KATHERINE: Extraordinary. One might be in Bokhara or Tiflis
or Afghanistan.
[*The bells become louder*]
Except for the bicycles. How many -
[*He holds up two fingers.*]
GURDJIEFF: Hundred.
KATHERINE: You bought two hundred bicycles?
[*There is frantic ringing, and sounds of a collision.*
KATHERINE *smiles and turns from the window.*]
I'm a little tired from the train. I'd like to go back to the
house and unpack.
GURDJIEFF: Your trunk is here.
KATHERINE: I don't understand.
GURDJIEFF: This where you stay.
KATHERINE: Above the cowshed?
GURDJIEFF: Not like cows?
KATHERINE: Well, yes, but . . .
GURDJIEFF: While you are at Institute for Harmonious Develop-
ment of Man you be same as other students.
KATHERINE: Of course. I'm . . . very fond of cows.
GURDJIEFF: You sleep near stairs. Breathe warm breath com-
ing up.
KATHERINE: And the smell.

GURDJIEFF: This special place. Made for me. I make exception
   to put you here.

KATHERINE: Oh. . . Then I'm honoured.

   [*She looks about with more attention.*]

   It's a kind of Persian pattern, isn't it? On the walls . . .
   Birds . . .and flowers . . .and butterflies . . . who painted
   them?

GURDJIEFF: My pig keeper. He was artist in Russia.

KATHERINE: It's charming.

   [*She shivers slightly.*]

   And I think it might be warmer than in the house.

GURDJIEFF: Healthy for you.

   [*He taps his head.*]

   You too much up here. Must become one of those down there.

KATHERINE: A cow?

GURDJIEFF: Tomorrow sit in kitchen. Peel carrots.

KATHERINE: I hope you're not intending I become a vegetable
   as well.

GURDJIEFF: You are Katherine Mansfield. Famous lady writer.
   That is big problem to overcome. But *haida,* we fix.

KATHERINE: Haida?

GURDJIEFF: Top speed!

KATHERINE: Mr Gurdjieff, I don't see that as my problem. My
   problem is that I wish to continue being a writer and I no
   longer have the energy to do my work.

GURDJIEFF: Writing not important.

KATHERINE: It is to me!

GURDJIEFF: Must learn to live in body again. English people's
   consciousness all up here -

   [*He taps his head.*]

KATHERINE: I'm not English.

GURDJIEFF: American's down here.

   [*He pats his groin.*]

KATHERINE: I'm from New Zealand.

GURDJIEFF: Then we see what you are. [*Touching her head.*]
   Here?

   [*He moves his hand down her body.*]

   Or here?

   [KATHERINE *recoils.*]

   [*Amused*] You be my New Zealand guinea pig.

KATHERINE: Tomorrow - apart from peeling carrots, am I to have any other sort of lesson from you?

GURDJIEFF: I go to Paris tomorrow. Can't run school, take care of students and many relatives without money.

KATHERINE: What do you do in Paris?

GURDJIEFF: I have factory makes false eyelashes, run two restaurants, sell carpets. Many ways smart man can make money.

[*He watches her.*]

You think of me as teacher? Guru?

KATHERINE: You have disciples.

GURDJIEFF: In life play many roles. Money 'sheared' from sheep is for school, yes. But need other money for self and relatives from Russia. Since the revolution I have very large family.

[*Pause.*]

You think I am phony? Very good American word 'phony'. I learn from student.

KATHERINE: I was warned in London to stay away from you.

GURDJIEFF: Good advice. Why you not take? Make you miserable. Unhappy. You wish that?

KATHERINE: No one here seems unhappy.

GURDJIEFF: Eyes open, see nothing.

KATHERINE: What does that mean?

GURDJIEFF: It means you are asleep. Most people are asleep. This why you come here: to wake up.

[*He moves to go.*]

We have evening meal seven o'clock. After have lessons in Study House until one, two. If you are tired Lidia will bring you back here. In morning Madame Ostrovsky brings you fresh milk. She see you drink all of it.

[*He exits.* KATHERINE *takes out a letter. As she reads she begins to cough.*]

SCENE THREE

London, 1922. KATHERINE *sits in the garden reading the letter.*
MURRY *comes out of the house behind her, registers that she
is coughing, and turns to go in again.* KATHERINE *sees him.*

KATHERINE: I should have been born a crocodile. It's the only
    creature, according to Sir Thomas Browne, that doesn't
    cough.

MURRY: You shouldn't be out here.

KATHERINE: I thought I'd wait until Lawrence had gone. [*Mock-
    ingly*] 'How are you, Katherine?' . . . 'Oh, I'm just dandy,
    thank you, Lawrence.'

MURRY: You didn't ask after his health either.

KATHERINE: Because he's terrified. Every time he sees me he
    sees his own illness looking back at him.

MURRY: Poor devil. One doesn't like to think of Lawrence being
    ill.

KATHERINE: One doesn't like to think of anyone being ill!

MURRY: You'd better come in. It's too cold for you out here.
    [KATHERINE *remains where she is.*]

KATHERINE: I've been thinking about Mother.

MURRY: Please come in.

KATHERINE: She told me once she wished she hadn't married,
    had been an explorer instead.
    [*She smiles, remembering.*]
    The rivers of China, she thought . . . I asked her what she
    knew about the rivers of China, because Mother knew no
    geography whatever - less than a child of ten. She agreed
    she knew nothing, then she said, 'But I can *feel* the sort of
    hat I should wear!' I miss the country, don't you? It's wick-
    ed to live among stones and chimneys.

MURRY: We could rent a house in Cornwall for the summer.

KATHERINE: Cornwall?

MURRY: I've heard of a place near St Ives.

KATHERINE: Near the Lawrences.

MURRY: Yes, as a matter of fact.

KATHERINE: How near?

MURRY: Next door. He says it's just right for us. Katherine's tower, he calls it.

KATHERINE: Wants to lock me up, does he?

MURRY: It's just a figure of speech, darling. It isn't really a tower.

KATHERINE: You know all about it, then?

MURRY: He says it's very cheap and we could let this place and probably get four guineas a week for it.

KATHERINE: But all our things are here!

MURRY: We let it furnished. *Five* guineas!

KATHERINE: I don't like Cornwall. And Frieda frightens me. I don't want to spend our entire summer together ducking to avoid flat-irons and saucepans.

MURRY: We wouldn't have to visit every day.

KATHERINE: Gods, I should hope not.

> [*Pause.*]

I spend every winter away from you. At least in summer we could be together.

MURRY: We are together.

KATHERINE: No wonder Virginia can write. Her roof over her, her possessions round, her man within call -

MURRY: I'm *here!*

KATHERINE: You planned this with Lawrence!

MURRY: We discussed it, that's all.

KATHERINE: Jack, there are books appearing in the house you don't show me or discuss with me. If I don't ask about them you just put them away. You know I can seldom go out, hardly ever get to a bookshop -

MURRY: I'm sorry.

KATHERINE: I'm scarcely part of your life at all now. Katherine's tower? I don't need bricks and mortar to feel shut away. I think you're only really happy when I'm not here.

MURRY: That's not true!

KATHERINE: You bloom in winter. Positively put forth leaves and branches. It's in your letters: the relief! In every line.

MURRY: I'm better at expressing myself on paper.

KATHERINE: Yes. You're not being 'driven distracted'.

MURRY: You pick me up on things but don't remember the good times.

KATHERINE: I do remember. I've nothing else to do but remember. It's at the root of my not getting better. My mind isn't controlled. It's not just physical. I have to cure my thoughts as well.

MURRY: That's nonsense.

KATHERINE: Is it? [*Quietly*] You never hold me. I've seen you when I cough -

[*She stops herself. A pause.*]

Do you think we go on?

MURRY: [*bleakly*] There has to be more than just this.

KATHERINE: That's the difference between us. I find 'just this' extraordinary. I'd like to keep in it for a while.

[*Pause.*]

Little things: sweeping out the house, picking a rose for the table, hurrying off just in time to meet the train that tumbles you into my arms . . . going into your room and putting my arm around you and saying, 'Look, there's that diamond of light in the shutter!'

[*She shivers.*]

I know quite well the truth is that I'm sitting at the window and the house is burning up behind me.

[MURRY *puts his arms around her. He holds her a moment until she moves away.*]

I think I may don the appropriate hat and head for China.

MURRY: You mean Cornwall?

KATHERINE: You can take the 'phallic insouciance'. I can't.

[*She hands* MURRY *the letter.*]

MURRY: Gurdjieff? Oh, Jesus!

KATHERINE: Not quite. But close enough from what his disciples tell me.

MURRY: Disciples? Halfwits! How to be a super-woman by taking care of pigs!

KATHERINE: I'm thinking of going there.

MURRY: Where?

KATHERINE: Fontainebleau.

MURRY: Don't be ridiculous. The man's preposterous. He's a fake!

KATHERINE: Who told you that? Aleister Crowley?

MURRY: He should know. They're two of a kind: evil.

KATHERINE: From what I hear Gurdjieff is the one man who understands the relationship between body and spirit. Doctors only treat half.

MURRY: He also claims he can kill a yak ten miles away. I mean, really, why bother? [*Reading*] 'Hydrotherapy, electrotherapy, dietotherapy' - Oh, Wig, you're not serious? . . . 'Duliotherapy'! What in God's name is that?

KATHERINE: I believe it's something to do with submission to the will of the Master.

MURRY: 'Cosomological mechanics'. . . 'gymnastics' - now I know you can't be serious - 'Oriental dancing' . . . 'exercises for the development of will and concentration'. That'll be the 'Stop' exercise. I've heard about that. [*Shouting*] STOP!

　　　[KATHERINE *ignores him.*]

You'll have to do better than that. The cats froze and you didn't.

KATHERINE: I said I was *thinking* about it.

MURRY: [*reading*] 'Man has become an uprooted creature, unable to adapt himself to life and alien to all the circumstances of his present existence.'

　　　[*He looks up.*]

Well, my alienated creature: you don't need it.

　　　[*He tears it up.*]

KATHERINE: What do I need, Jack?

MURRY: Rest.

KATHERINE: Gods! I get up at eleven, come downstairs until two, go up and lie on my bed until five and it's time to get back in it again. I've been *resting* for five years! I feel like a beetle shut in a book. If I rest any more I'll be dead! You may as well write my obituary. . . If you haven't already.

MURRY: Don't. I can't bear it.

KATHERINE: *You* can't bear it. I think every day has to be the last day of living like this.

MURRY: I'm not made of whipcord and steel. I know you can't help it, but don't.

KATHERINE: If I can't talk to you who can I talk to?

MURRY: I try, Katherine -

KATHERINE: This illness is turning me into a woman and that's the last thing you need.

[*A silence.*]

MURRY: When did you become so cruel?

KATHERINE: I think it was when that nice man in Switzerland told me I might have a chance. Yes, I think that was when.

MURRY: I don't know what to say any more. It's hopeless my saying anything. You know I love you. I haven't changed. You have.[*Quietly*] All I know is, if you go under so shall I.

[KATHERINE *stares at him. There is a silence.*]

KATHERINE: I'm going to Gurdjieff.

MURRY: What?

KATHERINE: Whatever he tells me to do, I'll do.

MURRY: He can't tell you anything! He's not a doctor.

KATHERINE: No. He isn't a doctor.

[*She looks at him*]

And he has one other advantage. He isn't you.

[*She turns and leaves him. After a moment* MURRY *exits.*]

SCENE FOUR

A figure lies in a bed, its identity concealed by bandages cover-ing the head. The hands are encased in padded mittens to prevent interference with the bandages. WAYNE *enters wearing overalls and carrying a bucket and mop. He studies some words he has scribbled on a length of toilet paper.*

WAYNE: Much have I travelled in the realms of gold. [*Puzzled*] Perhaps it's a song. [*Singing*]

> Much have I tra-a-v-e-lled
> In the realms of gold. . .

[*To the figure in the bed*] How's that for a piece of graffiti? Wonder who put it there? I'd give my right arm to find out. [*Reading*] And many good. . . 'Goodly'? [*Frustrated*] Good-ly what? Some dumb bastard comes along and scratches it out. Shouldn't be allowed in public toilets. Vandals! Get 'em out! [*To the figure*] When are you going to wake up, eh? Everyone else has heard my repertoire six times. [*Shouting*] *So wake up, eh?*

[*He swings the mop wildly in a passion of frustration. The figure doesn't respond.*]

I want to know the rest of it! I want to know! I want to know!

[*He stops and looks carefully around. He dips his hand in the bucket of water, then raises his hand above the figure, moving it slowly, ritualistically, in a line from head to foot, small drops of water falling on the body. He looks furtively around, then picks up his mop again.*]

And *you* can't tell me. No one can! If I gnawed your foot like a *rat* you couldn't tell me!

[*He stops abruptly and snaps to attention, mop at his shoulder like a rifle.*]

Wayne Shute. [*Solemnly*] 'Remember me. Remember me when I am gone away.'

[*He does an about turn.*]

'Far away into the silent land. . .'

[*He starts to march off, remembers the bucket and stops.*]

Shit.

[*He picks up the bucket and slouches off. The figure remains.*]

SCENE FIVE

Fontainebleau, 1922 : The gallery above the cowshed.
KATHERINE *writes a letter. She picks up an apple and absent-mindedly bites into it.*

KATHERINE: Dear Jack, It is intensely cold here - as cold as Switzerland. But it does not matter in the same way. One has not the time to think about it. I spent the winter afternoon yesterday peeling carrots - masses of carrots. People were running in and out of the kitchen. Portions of the first pig we have killed were on the table and greatly admired. Coffee was roasting in the oven.

[*Pause.*]

Madam Ostrovsky walks about like a queen exactly. Nina, a big girl in a black apron, pounds at things in mortars. A man in the scullery cleans pots. The dog barks and lies on the floor worrying a hearthbrush. A little girl comes in with a bouquet of leaves. Mr Gurdjieff strides in, takes up a handful of shredded cabbage and eats it. . . There are at least twenty pots on the stove.

[*Pause.*]

Lawrence is someone who could understand this place, but his pride would keep him back. No one person here is more important than another. There is only one student, Asanov, I plan to steer myself away from. But he infuriates everyone. I suspect this is why Mr Gurdjieff keeps him here.

[*Pause. She doesn't notice as* GURDJIEFF *enters silently and watches her.*]

It is absolutely brilliantly sunny - a deep blue sky. But cold - colder and colder. I shall be glad when the year has turned. I live in my fur coat. I gird it on like my heavenly armour and wear it ever night and day. But I must get some galoshes. My foot-gear is ridiculous when I am where I was today - round about the pigsty. It is noteworthy that the pigs have of themselves divided their sty into two; one, the clean part, they keep clean and sleep in. This makes one look at pigs with a different eye. One must be impartial, even about them, it seems.

[*She looks up.* GURDJIEFF *indicates the pages of writing paper.*]

GURDJIEFF: What is here?

[KATHERINE *remains silent.*]

Yes?

[*She writes on a sheet of paper and holds it out to him. He reads what she has written.*]

How many?

[*She holds up two fingers.*]

Hundred?

[*She smiles and shakes her head.*]

Two days. Good. You speak now. What are you doing?

KATHERINE: I'm writing to my husband.

GURDJIEFF: No letters.

KATHERINE: But if I can't talk and I'm not able to write stories, what am I meant to do?

GURDJIEFF: Eat.

[*She stares.*]

Apple.

KATHERINE: Why?

GURDJIEFF: [*Pointing to it*] Eat!

[KATHERINE *picks up the remainder of the apple and bites into it.* GURDJIEFF *watches until she has finished it.*]

Good?

KATHERINE: I wouldn't say I enjoyed it, no.

GURDJIEFF: Before you not taste at all. Must think what you do.

[*He takes her letter, screws it up and tosses it away.*]

You take energy from more important work.

KATHERINE: There was a list there of things you told me to write about myself. Don't you want to read it?

GURDJIEFF: List was for you. I already know Katherine Mansfield. Some day I introduce you.

KATHERINE: Mr Gurdjieff, I've been at Fontainebleau more than a week now. When is my treatment going to start?

GURDJIEFF: Has started.

KATHERINE: But I don't seem to be doing anything except peeling carrots and onions and watching the others dancing or digging ditches. I thought I came here to find out who I am?

GURDJIEFF: Perhaps nothing to find.

KATHERINE: Then why am I here?

GURDJIEFF: That is good question. Must keep asking yourself.

KATHERINE: I'm asking you.

GURDJIEFF: But it is you who must find answer.

KATHERINE: How?

GURDJIEFF: First must wake up. When you get up from bed in morning, you think you wake up?

KATHERINE: Of course. I know the difference between sleeping and waking.

GURDJIEFF: For you, no difference. Have never been awake.

KATHERINE: Then what are you? A dream? . . . A nightmare?

GURDJIEFF: You will know when wake up what I am.

[*He picks up a photograph of* MURRY.]

This husband?

KATHERINE: Yes, that's Jack.

GURDJIEFF: Cute.

[*He watches her reaction.*]

Very good American word, cute.

KATHERINE: Handsome. The word you are looking for is handsome.

GURDJIEFF: Many men think he is 'handsome' too.

KATHERINE: I suppose they do. Lawrence, certainly. D.H. Lawrence.

GURDJIEFF: You are lonely without husband?

KATHERINE: I'm lonely without him.

[*Pause.*]

I'm lonely with him. It's funny - I feel older than Jack now. As if I'd somehow skipped decades, become very old and everyone I knew had died, and I think of them, remember them as they are now, but I've become utterly changed. And Jack senses it. Now he talks like a young man to an older woman.

GURDJIEFF: [*returning the photograph*] Where is?

KATHERINE: Now? Reading 'Jacques le Fataliste', tramping the English countryside at weekends looking for a farm we'll never live on, putting pen to paper with the sole intention of killing me -

[*She stops.*]

Have you hypnotised me? I've heard you do that.

[GURDJIEFF *makes no response.*]

In any case, I'm here to remove the masks, am I not?

[*She picks up a review copy of a new book.*]

A Gift of the Dusk: the Journal of a Tubercular Patient. . .
Normally he sends me novels to review.

GURDJIEFF: Perhaps he think it help you.

KATHERINE: He thought it would help his magazine. Or rather he didn't think. Not about me. Not for one instant. Christ! . . . *His* suffering! *His* nerves! He's 'not made of whipcord and steel'. When I got ill it was a punishment - for *him!*

[KATHERINE *is breathless.* GURDJIEFF *pours a glass of water but does not give it to her. Instead he holds it between his palms as if warming it.*]

GURDJIEFF: You are on different path now. Impossible husband understand.

KATHERINE: [*angrily*] Why?

GURDJIEFF: Most people believe have aim in life and going somewhere. Americans talk of 'going places'. But man who is asleep has no aim and is not going anywhere. First sign of waking up is when he realise this and does not know where to go.

[*He looks at her.*]

But you know, Katherine. You here. Now. With me. You pass first lampost.

[KATHERINE *begins to cough.*]

KATHERINE: I want Jack. . .

[GURDJIEFF *concentrates on the glass he is holding.*]

I want to get well and go back to him.

[*She puts a hand to her chest, gasping*]

GURDJIEFF: Enough now. Time is breath. Don't waste.

KATHERINE: [*terrified*] What?

[*She looks at him in panic.*]

I can't breathe -

[GURDJIEFF *goes to her with the glass.*]

GURDJIEFF: Drink.

[*She tries to push it away.*]

Drink it!

[*He puts the glass in her hand and holds it to her lips. She swallows.*]

All of it.

[KATHERINE *obeys.*]

It is good you show this anger. This using emotional centre properly, not mixing with intellectual centre, which is bad habit with you. This why I say not write letters now.

[*The glass is empty.* KATHERINE'S *breathing is steady. She looks at the glass in puzzlement, then at* GURDJIEFF.]

KATHERINE: I don't understand.

[*She stares at him*]

Who are you? What are you?

[*He smiles.*]

GURDJIEFF: Perhaps devil.

KATHERINE: What was it? With the water . . . What did you do?

GURDJIEFF: How many doctors you see, Katherine?

> [*She is silent.*]

How many? [*Sharply*] Truth, please!

KATHERINE: [*reluctantly*] About twenty.

> [*Pause.*]

They all said the same thing. All but one. 'Get well? Of course you will. We'll put you right in no time!' [*Wryly*] The miracle never came near happening.

GURDJIEFF: Ah. You expect miracle.

> [KATHERINE *stares at the glass, then at* GURDJIEFF.]

KATHERINE: I've felt more and more lately that there's a whole world into which we're received if we can just yield to it. With all that we know, how much do we not know? I used to think I might know all but some mysterious core. But now I believe just the opposite. The unknown is far greater than the known. The known is only a shadow. I believe the real cause of my illness is not my lungs, but something else. If I could find that something else and cure it, all the rest would heal.

> [*Pause.*]

I believe you can do what I've dreamed might be done: cure my soul.

> [*They exit.*]

SCENE SIX

The ward. AUDRA *and* RAHEL *enter wearing white coats. They approach the bandaged figure in the bed and look down at it.*

AUDRA: Young?

RAHEL: Late twenties or thereabouts. Early thirties.

AUDRA: A mess? [*Quickly*] Nothing you couldn't put right, I'm sure.

RAHEL: Check it out. You're the doctor now.

[AUDRA *untapes the end of the bandage covering the head*.]

Just be careful what you say. The mind tends to register it.

AUDRA: [*as she unwraps*]   You believe that?

RAHEL: As a surgeon I err on the safe side. 'There are more things in heaven and earth - '

AUDRA: Please. Don't you start quoting things too.

RAHEL: Been seeing our erudite infant again, have we? The talking book.

AUDRA: I can't escape him, Rahel. Every time I come off duty, there he is.

RAHEL: And there *you* are. You could be getting fond of him.

[*The figure moans.* RAHEL *returns her attention to the patient*.]

You've got me breaking my own rule.

AUDRA: Sorry.

RAHEL: So. The moment of truth arrives.

[*She leans closer as* AUDRA *removes the final wrapping. The figure puts a mittened hand to it's face.* RAHEL *restrains it*.]

RAHEL: Don't touch. Don't spoil my handiwork.

AUDRA: I haven't seen the original of course, but I'd say you've done a brilliant job.

RAHEL: I'm very pleased.

AUDRA: You're an artist. [*Bending closer*] Extraordinary. . .

[*There is a silence as* AUDRA *examines the face*.]

I've never seen anything like it. Hardly any swelling or bruising. . . relatively minimal scarring. . .

[*She straightens, staring at* RAHEL.]

Almost impossible in such a short time.

[*Pause*.]

What have you done, Rahel?

RAHEL: [*turning to leave*] I'll look in again later.

AUDRA: I want an answer!

RAHEL: [*facing her*] The healing was greatly accelerated by the hypnosis I gave.

AUDRA: Hypnosis is against the rules, Rahel!

RAHEL: Not my rules.

AUDRA: It's too unpredictable! It's dangerous!

RAHEL: Don't worry. I'm in control. If I've done as well as I think I have, there's no way he could be a danger. That's the beauty of him.

[*The* MAN *groans.*]

AUDRA: You must be crazy to take a risk like that. You'll never get away with it. Someone will notice.

RAHEL: *I'm* not going to say anything.

[*The* MAN *tries to speak.* RAHEL *goes to him.*]

Don't be alarmed.

MAN: Who are you? Where am I?

RAHEL: You're in a hospital. Don't worry. You're quite alright now. In fact I'm very pleased with you.

MAN: What's happened. . . [*Louder, panicky*] What's happened to my voice?

RAHEL: Nothing's happened to your voice. The rest of you may be a little weak, but you'll soon mend.

MAN: How did -

RAHEL: Please. Don't touch your face.

MAN: How did I get here?

AUDRA: You were brought here in an ambulance.

MAN: An ambulance . . . ? What's happened to me?

AUDRA: You were in an accident of some sort. We don't know what. They found you wandering in the Botanical Gardens.

MAN: Where?

RAHEL: Don't try to talk now. Rest.

MAN: I don't understand. Why am I here?

RAHEL: No more questions.

MAN: Get me a doctor! At once! I don't want nurses. Fetch someone who can tell me what's going on!

AUDRA: We are doctors. I'm Dr Audra, and this is Dr Rahel who repaired your face.

MAN: [*terrified*] My face? What's wrong with my face?

AUDRA: Nothing at all now . . . [*Coldly*] Thanks to Dr Rahel.

MAN: What have you done to me ? I want to see! Now! At once!

AUDRA: Relax.

MAN: Now!

[RAHEL *produces a mirror. The* MAN *tries to snatch it from her but is prevented by the mittens on his hands.*

AUDRA *watches stonily as* RAHEL *holds it for him. A moment of adjustment before he is able to see his face clearly. He stares, shaken.*]
My God. . .

RAHEL: I know. It's a normal reaction. It takes a little time to adjust to a new face.

MAN: There's been a mistake . . . What's happened to me? How did I get like this?

AUDRA: You were in an accident -

MAN: An accident doesn't do this!

RAHEL: I did the best I could with what remained.

MAN: Remained? What are you talking about? This isn't me!
[*He tries in vain to uncover the rest of his body.*]

RAHEL: [*restraining him*] It's as close as I could get.

AUDRA: [*with a cold look at* RAHEL] Dr Rahel is an expert.

MAN: [*wildly*] An expert in what?

AUDRA: Plastic surgery.

MAN: I don't know what you're talking about! Get me Dr Manoukhin!

AUDRA: There's no Dr Manoukhin here.

MAN: Then send a message! Quickly, before I go out of my mind!

AUDRA: If you'll just tell us who this doctor is -

MAN: What day is this?

RAHEL: Thursday.

MAN: I should be there now. This is the day I have my X-rays.

AUDRA: X-rays? X-rays for what?

MAN: To irradiate my spleen. I have them every Thursday.

AUDRA: Every Thursday, do you? What else does this doctor prescribe?

MAN: Iodine injections. . . strychnine . . .

RAHEL: [*smiling*] I recommend a sedative, doctor.
[RAHEL *prepares a shot. The* MAN *stares at the needle in horror.*]

MAN: Oh, God, this is a nightmare! Let me wake up!
[AUDRA *holds his arm ready for* RAHEL *to administer the shot.*]
You're not real! You can't be!
[*He pulls his arm away from the approaching needle.*]

Wait. Listen to me! You'll find Manoukhin's address on a card with my things - Where are my things? What have you done with them?

AUDRA: Your clothes are right here by your bed.

MAN: Then find Manoukhin's address!

[AUDRA *picks up the* MAN'*s belongings. She holds up a pair of denims and a shirt.*]

What are those?

AUDRA: They're yours.

MAN: Those are not my things.

AUDRA: I assure you these are the clothes you were wearing when you were brought in. You had socks but no shoes.

MAN: I wouldn't be seen dead in an outfit like that. Not even as fancy dress! I want my own things!

AUDRA: [*searching*] Nothing in the pockets.

MAN: I'm insane. Or you're insane. Oh God, help me to wake up!

RAHEL: I think sleep would be more in order.

[RAHEL *holds the needle aloft.*]

MAN: When I wake up will I be myself again?

AUDRA: Hold still.

MAN: I want to be the way I was!

RAHEL: We can't promise that, but you will adjust.

MAN: [*shouting*] No!

[AUDRA *holds him down.*]

I want to go back! I want to be who I was! Help me somebody! Help me!

[RAHEL *administers the shot.*]

[*sobbing*] I was a woman. . . ! I was a woman. . . ! [*Fading*] I want to wake up. . . I was a woman. . .

AUDRA: [*to* RAHEL] Coffee?

[*The look she directs at* RAHEL *is not sociable, but cold. They exit.*]

SCENE SEVEN

Fontainebleau, 1922. GURDJIEFF *continues* KATHERINE's *treatment.*

KATHERINE: My voice has gone. I've become no one. Mute. Empty.

GURDJIEFF: In order to become something, must first become nothing.

KATHERINE: But I was someone. I was Katherine Mansfield.

GURDJIEFF: You wish to leave your darkness?

KATHERINE: If the Grand Lama of Tibet said he could help me I'd follow him.

GURDJIEFF: There was no Katherine Mansfield. She did not exist. Repeat.

KATHERINE: But that isn't true!

GURDJIEFF: Repeat.

    [KATHERINE *is silent.*]

Okay. You find Grand Lama of Tibet. Don't bother Gurdjieff.

KATHERINE: There was no Katherine Mansfield. She did not exist.

GURDJIEFF: And now?

KATHERINE: There is no Katherine Mansfield. She does not exist.

GURDJIEFF: Good. Another face.

KATHERINE: Oh no. No more!

GURDJIEFF: Ugly face now. Haida! Top speed!

    [KATHERINE *makes a face.*]

You call that ugly face? Here is ugly face -

    [*He pulls a hideous face.* KATHERINE *smiles.*]

Okay.

    [KATHERINE *hesitates.*]

GURDJIEFF: Top speed!

    [*She makes a face.*]

Not ugly. Again!

    [*She tries again.*]

Good. We get rid of mask.

KATHERINE: I'm still an artist.

GURDJIEFF: You are nothing.

KATHERINE: I am someone who sat down to write every day at a yellow table. I did exist.

GURDJIEFF: This is wrong.

KATHERINE: I have books to prove it.

GURDJIEFF: Books written and created in sleep.

KATHERINE: By me.

GURDJIEFF: A machine.

KATHERINE: I'm flesh and blood. I'm real. I exist!

GURDJIEFF: Everything you think you know about Katherine Mansfield is false. You are series of imaginary events.

KATHERINE: If I'm not Katherine Mansfield, who am I?

GURDJIEFF: You have dozens of selves, all calling themselves 'Katherine Mansfield'. Perhaps many as one thousand.

KATHERINE: I sound like the proprietor of some dubious hotel who's registered too many guests, all calling themselves 'Smith'.

GURDJIEFF: You have no 'I'. If you say 'I' today and 'I' again tomorrow these two different people. Must work here to create one self. One 'I'....Who are you?

KATHERINE: [tiredly] I don't know.

GURDJIEFF: Who does not know?

KATHERINE: I don't.

GURDJIEFF: You have no 'I' to know, or not know, anything.

KATHERINE: Then what is the answer?

GURDJIEFF: What is the question?

KATHERINE: It's impossible to ask because it's impossible to formulate!

GURDJIEFF: Also impossible for you to know anything.

KATHERINE: [losing patience] Then what am I doing here?

GURDJIEFF: Already tell you, this is question must keep asking yourself.

KATHERINE: Yes, I can quite see why. But how am I to ask it if I have no self to ask? There's a contradiction there.

GURDJIEFF: Contradictions important in the work. They force pupil to discover for himself what is true.

KATHERINE: I suspect I've just made that discovery.

GURDJIEFF: Yes?

KATHERINE: I need a psychoanalyst.
GURDJIEFF: Only fuller developed person can use psycho-
   analyst. Simple machine like you need mechanic.
KATHERINE: [*bitterly*] Are you qualified?
   [GURDJIEFF *exits*. KATHERINE *follows*.]

SCENE EIGHT

The ward. The MAN *gazes at his reflection in the mirror,
balanced between his mittened hands.* WAYNE *enters, excited-
ly waving another length of toilet paper.*

WAYNE: Great news! I found some more in the same hand-
   writing! The next words are probably 'states and kingdoms',
   whatever that means.
MAN: [*vaguely*] What?
WAYNE: That's right - I forgot. You were asleep when I got
   the first words. [*Looking more closely at the* MAN]. You're
   still asleep.

>   Much have I travelled in the realms of gold,
>   And many goodly states and kingdoms seen.

   That makes sense, doesn't it?
   [*The* MAN *begins to speak softly.* WAYNE *turns to listen.*]
MAN: Round many western islands have I been
                   Which bards in fealty to Apollo hold.

   [WAYNE *lets the paper fall.*]
WAYNE: That's part of it?
MAN: Of course that's part of it.
WAYNE: Did you write it?
MAN: [*amused*] Did I write it? Would that I had.
   [*He returns to his contemplation of himself in the mir-
   ror.*]
WAYNE: Did you put it there?
MAN: [*looking round.*] I'm sorry?

WAYNE: Did you put it there? On the wall in the toilet? [*Realising*] No, you couldn't have. Unless you're just pretending you can't walk.

MAN: I haven't walked since nineteen twenty, except to a taxi and back.

WAYNE: Nineteen twenty? What are you on? They got you doped to the eyeballs?

     [*Pause.*]

You're not making it up, are you?

MAN: Making what up?

WAYNE: Those incredible words.

MAN: 'On First Looking into Chapman's Homer' by John Keats.

WAYNE: John? That was written by a man?

MAN: Of course.

WAYNE: Of course? Are you crazy? Of course? Where did you get it from?

MAN: I think I first read it in Palgrave's Golden Treasury when I was about thirteen. But I liked Shelley more.

WAYNE: Shelley? Who was she?

MAN: He.

WAYNE: Are you kidding me?

    [*The* MAN *recites as if it holds particular meaning for him.*]

MAN:

> Rarely, rarely comest thou,
> Spirit of Delight!
> Wherefore hast thou left me now
> Many a day and night?
> Many a weary night and day
> 'Tis since thou art fled away.
>
> How shall ever one like me
> Win thee back again?
> With the joyous and the free
> Thou wilt scoff at pain.
> Spirit false! thou hast forgot
> All but those who need thee not.

    [*He becomes aware that* WAYNE *is crying. The* MAN *reaches out a hand to him.* WAYNE *lifts his head.*]

WAYNE: How do you know that stuff?

MAN: Keats and Shelley?

WAYNE: [*fiercely*] Yes!

MAN: How do you not? I've heard you quoting Emily Dickinson, Elizabeth Barrett Browning -

WAYNE: They're women! You're talking about men. Men don't write poetry.

MAN: What about Robert?

WAYNE: Robert who?

MAN: *Robert* Browning.

WAYNE: He wasn't a writer. He was just married to her.

MAN: [*shouting*] Nurse! Nurse!

    [AUDRA *enters*]

  Nurse -

AUDRA: It's doctor.

MAN: Do get this fellow out of here.

AUDRA: Out, Wayne.

WAYNE: All I said was -

AUDRA: Out!

WAYNE: All I said was men don't write poetry.

AUDRA: You should know.

    [*Pause.*]

  That's all you said?

    [WAYNE *is silent.*]

  Do you have work to do in here?

WAYNE: Yes.

AUDRA: Then do it.

    [WAYNE *snatches the toilet paper from the floor and stalks off to begin cleaning.*]

MAN: Nurse - I mean doctor - I don't believe this is doing me the least bit of good. There doesn't seem much point in my staying.

AUDRA: I prefer to keep you under observation until your condition...stabilises. And until we find someone who can identify you.

MAN: I've told you who I am. Over and over.

AUDRA: We've found no trace of a Dr Manoukhin - nor the relative you mentioned. We did find a reference to a D.H.Lawrence in an encyclopaedia.

MAN: Then fetch him! If he's still in Italy send a telegram!

AUDRA: D.H.Lawrence died more than half a century ago.

[*A silence.*]

MAN: [*exploding*] Gods! How much more of this do I have to listen to? First you tell me I don't exist, that I'm not Katherine Mansfield, then you try to tell me my husband and friends don't exist either! You saw my photograph of Jack....

[WAYNE *stops cleaning.*]

WAYNE: Was he a poet?

MAN: He's a critic! Jack Middleton Murry: the most important literary critic in England today!

AUDRA: England?

MAN: [*impatiently*] I know perfectly well I'm not in England. I don't know whose body this is, my brain has no idea what's happening to me, and emotionally I'm scared out of my wits! But at least I know what country I'm in.

[*He throws back the covers and swings his legs over the side of the bed.*]

I've had enough mysticism. No amount of pulling ugly faces is going to make me less conscious of external appearances.

AUDRA: You look fine. Truly. It's a common anxiety after plastic surgery. You wake up with a brand new face but all the bad old feelings you had about yourself are still there.

[*The* MAN *turns to* WAYNE.]

MAN: Fetch me a stick.

WAYNE: I thought you said you couldn't walk?

MAN: I can if you fetch me a stick.

AUDRA: You don't need a stick.

MAN: [*ignoring* AUDRA] And find someone to accompany me on the train back to Paris. Telegram the Select Hotel.

WAYNE: Paris?

MAN: I prefer X-rays to inanity. I'm going back to Manoukhin. [*For* AUDRA*'s benefit.*] He's a real doctor.

AUDRA: [*drily*] I'm glad to hear it. I had my doubts for a moment.

MAN: Don't try and stop me.

AUDRA: I wouldn't dream of it. You've chosen a lovely day for your adventure. The weather's perfect. Sunny . . . and warm.

MAN: It's not snowing?

AUDRA: No, there's no snow.

MAN: I've been so cold. . . Colder and colder.

AUDRA: Let me show you.

MAN: I need a stick.

AUDRA: You can do it. A little walk to the window will do you good. I'll help you.

[*She helps the* MAN *up.*]

Wayne.

[WAYNE *takes the* MAN *'s other arm. They go to the window. The* MAN *'s arm goes to his eyes, shielding them.*]

MAN: [*confused*] The light . . . ! I've never seen such light.

AUDRA: It's December.

WAYNE: The middle of summer.

[*The* MAN *leans his forehead against the window.*]

MAN: Oh, God. . .

[AUDRA *studies him a moment.*]

AUDRA: [*briskly*] What was it you wanted? A train to Paris? Better get cracking. . . Mustn't be late!

[*The* MAN *doesn't move.*]

Come along!

MAN: [*to himself*] There's no train.

AUDRA: What was that?

MAN: No train . . .

AUDRA: Of course there's no train. Good. We're making sense, are we? How about popping back into bed now?

MAN: Help me.

[*The* MAN *raises his voice and shouts hoarsely.*]

Help me!

AUDRA: You've come this far, There's no reason why you can't -

MAN: [*shouting from the window*] *Help me!*

[AUDRA *pulls him away*]

AUDRA: That's enough. You'll cause an accident in Macquarie Street. Now. . . off you go.

[*The* MAN *takes a tentative step on his own.* AUDRA *applauds.*]

Good work. Keep going!

[*The* MAN *tries, but one leg refuses to function.*]

MAN: My leg -

[WAYNE *moves to assist him.*]

AUDRA: Leave him Wayne!

[*to the* MAN.]

You can do it.
> [*The* MAN *shuffles slowly to the bed, apparently in considerable pain. He collapses, hand to chest, gasping.*]

MAN: I can't breathe!

AUDRA: Of course you can breathe!
> [*She tries to push him back on the pillows.*]

Lie down.

MAN: [*resisting*] No. . . I have to sit up. My lungs -

AUDRA: There's nothing wrong with your lungs. We've done all the scans, conduction studies - there's not a sign of T.B.
> [*The* MAN *is gasping for breath.*]

MAN: My spine -

AUDRA: I've examined your spine.

MAN: I have a lump -

AUDRA: There's no evidence of a lump on your spine.

MAN: [*breathlessly*] Help me! . . . Please! I think I'm going to die.

WAYNE: Do something for him!

AUDRA: There's nothing wrong with him.
> [*The* MAN *goes into a paroxysm of coughing and drags the sheet to his lips.* WAYNE *reacts in panic .*]

WAYNE: You bloody help him!

AUDRA: How dare you order me -
> [*Blood appears on the sheet.*]

WAYNE: Do something!

MAN: Water -
> [AUDRA *pours a glass of water. The* MAN *gestures urgently to her to hold the glass to his lips. He drinks eagerly.*]

Thank you.
> [*He settles back and closes his eyes.* AUDRA *is puzzled.*]

AUDRA: You're all right now?

MAN: Of course.

WAYNE: What did you give him?

AUDRA: [*puzzled*] Just water.
> [*She looks at the* MAN.]

Open your mouth.
> [*She examines him.*]

I can't see anything.
> [*She turns to* WAYNE.]

Keep an eye on him, Wayne. I'm going to have a word
with Dr Rahel.

WAYNE: [*sarcastically*] No worries.

    [AUDRA *exits. As soon as they are alone* WAYNE *goes
to the* MAN.]

You sure you're all right?

MAN: There is no God or Heaven or help of any kind but love.
. . Get well, be happy - it's hopeless. Horror. . .

WAYNE: Who wrote that? Was it written by someone? Who
said it?

MAN: No one.

    [*A silence.* WAYNE *waits for more.*]

It's another world out there, isn't it?

WAYNE: You think so? Yes it is. You feel like an alien? So
do I.

MAN: More than anything I want to go home.

WAYNE: I can understand that. And I don't even know what
I mean by it. I live in a room and it isn't home. I live in
Australia - and it isn't home. I live on earth - and it isn't
home. With everyone I meet I feel alien. Except you. You're
weird, but you seem familiar. I catch myself imagining
you're from the real world. The one I dream about. The
one I'd pray existed, if there was anyone I knew to pray to.

MAN: Pray to God.

WAYNE: In secret, you mean?

MAN: Privately? Of course.

WAYNE: It goes against the official wisdom from H.D.

> O is it not enough to greet
> the red-rose
> for the red, red sweet of it?
> must we encounter
> with each separate flower,
> some god, some goddess?

    [*Anxiously*] You didn't mean it, did you?

MAN: Mean what?

WAYNE: What you said. About dying.

    [*The* MAN'*s eyes begin to close.*]

You said, 'I think I'm going to die.'

MAN: [*tired*] I'm sick of people dying who promise well...One doesn't want to join that crowd at all...

WAYNE: Good. Don't even think about it.

MAN: There's a great black bird flying over me ...and I'm so frightened he'll settle...so terrified...

WAYNE: Don't think about it. Forget about blackbirds. Don't think about anything. Only Keats and Shelley...'Spirit of Delight.'

　　[*The* MAN's *eyes close.*]

MAN: [*fading*] 'Spirit of Delight.'

　　[*He falls silent.*]

WAYNE: [*panicking*] You okay? [*Shaking him*] You okay?

　　[*He feels the* MAN's *pulse.*]

No pulse! There must be a pulse!

　　[*He finds it.*]

Asleep. Good.

　　[*Pause.*]

Just don't try anything stupid, mate. No blackbirds, okay? Or I'll make you sorry you were ever born... I'm going to sit here until you hatch, man. Until whoever you are puts its head out and says a *name*!

　　[*Lights fade on* WAYNE *and the* MAN,*who remain on stage. The back wall is lit.*]

SCENE NINE

RAHEL *writes on the wall in large letters using a spray can:'A MAN'S REACH'* AUDRA *enters.*

AUDRA: You're risking your job.

RAHEL: I don't measure myself by my job.

　　[*She adds 'SHOULD EXCEED HIS GRASP'.*]

AUDRA: The rules are there for a reason, Rahel.

RAHEL: What reason?

AUDRA: You know what happened in the past.

RAHEL: We know what we've been told.

AUDRA: Our words were taken from us. We were silenced. For centuries. We don't know our history. We'll never know.

RAHEL: Does that mean we should do the same to them? What does that make us?

AUDRA: It makes us safe.

RAHEL: It makes us liars.
   [*Pause.*]
What are you afraid of, Audra?

AUDRA: Nightmares. Bad dreams.

RAHEL: We all have those.

AUDRA: You don't have to continue with this. I kept quiet about the hypnosis. You could stop right now and I wouldn't say anything.

RAHEL: It's not in my power.

AUDRA: You use *their* words!

RAHEL: Beautiful words. Words you never dreamed of!

AUDRA: Illegal words! Criminal!

RAHEL: Okay. Report me. I don't need the hospital to continue my work.

AUDRA: Where will you go?

RAHEL: Somewhere where they won't find me.
   [*She grabs* AUDRA *and forces her round to face the wall.*]
Look at it, Audra. Look! The words won't kill you!
   [AUDRA *is forced to look. She takes it in. She breaks free, stepping back and staring at* RAHEL *as if seeing her clearly for the first time.*]

AUDRA: You'd put us at risk... [*Icy, condemning*] You're a danger...You want to bring back the Horror.
   [*She turns and goes swiftly out.* RAHEL *takes an unhurried look at her handiwork, then exits in the opposite direction.*]

SCENE TEN

Lights up on KATHERINE *and* GURDJIEFF, *as* WAYNE *continues his vigil over the* MAN.

KATHERINE: [*in a strong voice*]'I'.

GURDJIEFF: Where?

KATHERINE: In my chest, I think. I'm not sure.

GURDJIEFF: Again.

KATHERINE: 'I'.
    [*Pause.*]
That was in my head, I think.

GURDJIEFF: Put back in chest.

KATHERINE: 'I'.
    [*Pause.*]
That didn't seem to be anywhere. It was outside my head somewhere.

GURDJIEFF: Try again.

KATHERINE: 'I'. [*A hand on her chest*] Yes! I could feel it!

GURDJIEFF: Good. Whenever you think of this person you call 'I', must think where this 'I' is coming from and try to bring from one centre to another. Again.

KATHERINE: 'I'.
    [*The* MAN *echoes her.*]

MAN: 'I'.
    [WAYNE *straightens, staring at the* MAN.]

GURDJIEFF: Where?

KATHERINE: In my head.

GURDJIEFF: Chest.

KATHERINE: 'I'.

MAN: 'I'.

GURDJIEFF: Where?

KATHERINE: [*smiling*] Chest.

GURDJIEFF: Head.

KATHERINE: 'I'.

MAN: 'I'.
    [WAYNE *leans forward in alarm. The* MAN's *eyes are closed.*]

WAYNE: [*getting up*] Doctor?
    [*He hesitates, not sure whether to leave the* MAN *or not.*]
Doctor!

GURDJIEFF: [*to* KATHERINE] Stay with the head.

KATHERINE: 'I'.

MAN: 'I'.

WAYNE: Shit.

KATHERINE: 'I'.

MAN: 'I'.

> [AUDRA *enters*.]

WAYNE: [*dismayed*] Where's Dr Rahel?

AUDRA: Dr Rahel is no longer working here.

> [*She takes the* MAN's *pulse*.]

  No problems?

> [WAYNE *is silent, eyeing the* MAN *nervously*.]

GURDJIEFF: Try to remember yourself. Until you can remember yourself you do not exist.

WAYNE: He's frightened he's going to die.

AUDRA: Rubbish.

> [*She lifts the* MAN's *eyelid*.]

GURDJIEFF: Good. You work hard. Pass second lampost. Soon discover America!

AUDRA: Out like a light.

GURDJIEFF: And I have reward for you. Starting tomorrow you take care of pigs!

> [*He exits*.]

AUDRA: I'm going off duty now. You coming?

> [WAYNE *is still staring at the* MAN. *He appears not to hear her*.]

WAYNE: If only we knew who he was.

AUDRA: The police can't identify him. Are you ready?

WAYNE: Missing persons.

AUDRA: [*coldly*] There are no missing persons any more.

WAYNE: Not women.

AUDRA: I said I'm leaving now.

WAYNE: [*avoiding looking at her*] I think I might stay for a while.

> [AUDRA *stares*.]

AUDRA: Goodnight.

> [*Pause*.]

WAYNE: [*nervously*] Goodnight.

> [AUDRA *exits*. WAYNE *continues to brood over the* MAN. *He reaches out and smoothes the hair over the* MAN's *forehead*.]

KATHERINE: [*recalling*] 'Miss Mansfield is brilliant - she has, more conspicuously than any contemporary writer of fiction one calls to mind, a fine, infinitely inquisitive sen-

sibility... [*Critical, self-aware*]...A sensibility which finds
itself in the service of a mind often cynical, sometimes cruel
and always sophisticated.' [*Wryly*] I don't care a fig for
reviews, not I. Not much!

[*Pause.*]

'...The first short-story writer of genius who has appeared
this century ...To read her makes one glad to be alive and on
this shining planet.'

[*Pause.*]

'What a pleasure it is to think of all the years of writing Miss
Mansfield has before her.'

[KATHERINE *exits slowly with the aid of her stick.* WAYNE
has removed the mitt from one of the MAN *'s hands. He
sits holding the hand in his as the lights fade.*]

END OF ACT ONE

ACT TWO

SCENE ONE

The words 'MY LORD FOOL' have replaced 'A MAN'S REACH SHOULD EXCEED HIS GRASP'   A makeshift film studio. MATTHEW *and* MARK *are setting up.* MATTHEW *turns a light on, illuminating the subject, a* GIRL. *The* GIRL *sits cross-legged on the floor. Her hands are tied behind her and her mouth is gagged. There is a blindfold covering her eyes.*

MARK: I'll set the blondie here.

MATTHEW: We'll need some fill...Get me a couple of red-heads for the sides. And get some spun while you're there.
    [*He feels his pockets.*]
    I'm out of cigarettes.
        [MARK *tosses him a pack as he passes.*]
    I don't know how you can smoke these. These are the worst.
    They'll kill you.

MARK: [*returning with the lights*] What are we going to do with her?

MATTHEW: I'm thinking.
        [*They contemplate the* GIRL. *After a pause.*]
    The bath.

MARK: How?

MATTHEW: We fill it about two-thirds full, balance her on the plank, and when you've finished with her you pull a lever.

MARK: What lever?

MATTHEW: I don't know! You're the handyman! We'll rig something up. You pull a lever, the board tilts down, and her head's underwater.

MARK: Where am I?

MATTHEW: You're on top of her.

MARK: I'll get wet!

MATTHEW: So?

MARK: I'm not crazy about it.

MATTHEW: It'll work!

MARK: It's been done.

MATTHEW: Everything's been done.

MARK: Where's the drama? Wouldn't it be better if instead of her going under, the water was coming up slowly and we're tight on her face?

MATTHEW: That could work.

MARK: We can only do it once so make up your mind.

MATTHEW: I like my idea.

MARK: Why don't we ask her?

MATTHEW: Yeah. Ask her how she wants it.

    [*He takes a light reading.*]

Let her get a look at it first. Don't take the gag off. I want the eyes. The eyes are lovely. Very expressive. Speaking eyes, we used to call them.

    [MARK *goes behind the* GIRL *and unties the blindfold. He steps back. Dead silence while the* GIRL *takes it in. Her gaze travels slowly from left to right, then swings slowly back to focus on* MATTHEW. *Lighting changes.* MATTHEW *freezes.*

MARK: Matthew?

    [*There is no response.* MARK *walks round the* GIRL *and up to* MATTHEW. *He shakes him.* MATTHEW *is rigid.* MARK *turns to look at the* GIRL. *Blackout. The* GIRL'*s voice begins in the darkness. Gradually the lights come up.* MATTHEW *and* MARK *are gone. The* GIRL *is standing, hands free, without the gag.*]

GIRL: It was a hot night. She was ironing a pair of shorts for the beach tomorrow. There were no cigarettes. She went down to the corner. A car stopped. A door opened. Two men. She remembered thinking she'd left the iron on.

    [*Lights slowly come up on the* MAN *in a wheelchair, watching a video with* WAYNE.]

Some said the Look was a myth come to life: Medusa, mother of all the gods, who is past, present, and future; all that has been, that is, and that will be. It was an evolutionary leap, the ultimate weapon, which rendered all previous weapons obsolete. Men walked about with their eyes downcast as women had been trained to do in earlier cultures -

    [WAYNE *turns it off.*]

MAN: Extraordinary.

WAYNE: It can't be the first time you've seen a video.

MAN: I must make a note of this. . .'A car stopped. A door opened. Two men. . . . 'I don't know anyone who writes like that. Mere skin and bone. . . Is there much of this sort of thing?

WAYNE: Comes on every channel.

[*He offers the* MAN *a lolly and is refused.*]

MAN: Channel?

WAYNE: Everywhere. Cinemas, parks, stadiums. They have Medusa festivals, pageants and things where they rejoice in the Look.

MAN: This is a tawdry little allegory. . .

WAYNE: Allegory?

MAN: [*impatiently*] Story.

WAYNE: It's not a story. It's real! If you've been Looked at you know it.

MAN: Yes, I'm sure.

WAYNE: You go into spasms, flip out on the floor. . . or turn to stone.

MAN: I've enjoyed our little chat but now I'd like to sleep.

WAYNE: It's hardly ever used anymore. [*Bitterly*] They don't need to. If we just had access to scientific knowledge I reckon we could figure it out. But they like to keep us stupid.

MAN: This is a strange way to cure one's soul. . .

WAYNE: I'm telling you this for a reason. Okay? I'm saying, be careful.

[*He starts to wheel the* MAN *off.*]

MAN: Were you here all night?

WAYNE: [*embarrassed*] I was hanging around for a while, yeah. Why?

MAN: [*to himself*] It's a dreadful thing to be alone. . .

[*They exit. Blackout.*]

SCENE TWO

Fontainebleau, 1922. The music by GURDJIEFF *and Thomas de Hartmann, 'Journey to Inaccessible Places,' is heard.* KATHERINE *performs a sequence of the* GURDJIEFF *movements. A spot reveals her in the surrounding blackness. The movement is slow, hypnotic, suggesting a prayer in motion. The lights come up to reveal other dancers as they move into a second sequence:* LIDIA, ASANOV *and* VERA. KATHERINE *breaks away from the group and sits watching them. The second sequence, which should not be long - about the same duration as* KATHERINE's *- is interrupted by the entrance of* GURDJIEFF *as* KATHERINE *stands to rejoin them.*

GURDJIEFF: Stop!
> [*They freeze.* ASANOV *cheats, swiftly adopting an easier pose.* GURDJIEFF *notes it but says nothing. He lights a cigarette and moves about examining them before strolling off. A silence, broken at last by* ASANOV.]

ASANOV: This is what I think happens. He takes his car, he drives to Paris, sells half a dozen carpets, he's sitting in a cafe and thinks, 'Something I have forgotten. What was it?'
> [*He sits down.*]

Today I have dug three trenches for the Turkish bath, planted six rows of cabbages and memorised nine Tibetan verbs since breakfast. He says to keep asking ourselves why we are here. This question becomes embarrassing.
> [KATHERINE'S *pose starts to cause her distress.* ASANOV *regards her without sympathy.*]

[*Imitating* GURDJIEFF'S *accent.*]   If water not reach one hundred degrees is not boiling. You must reach boiling point or you fall back again. [*In his normal accent*] . . . I don't think Mrs. Murry should try to reach boiling.

LIDIA: Why do you stay here, Asanov?

ASANOV: Why does Mrs Murry stay? We're not a hospital.
> [GURDJIEFF *enters behind* VERA.]

VERA: [*in an English upper-class accent*] The Master knows what he's doing.

[ASANOV *sees* GURDJIEFF.]

ASANOV: Do you? Tell us the point of the 'Stop' exercise, Vera.

VERA: To help us wake up and remember ourselves. Bring us out of our hypnosis.

GURDJIEFF: So, Vera. You are authority on the 'Stop' exercise? [*Pointing from* VERA *to* ASANOV] You pour from one empty vessel to another. Enough.

[*They unfreeze.*]

Lidia, take Mrs Murry back to house. Asanov, five more trenches for Turkish bath.

ASANOV: What!

GURDJIEFF: You dig, Asanov. Top speed. No more shovel. Use hands.

ASANOV: You're crazy!

[*He looks at* KATHERINE *being helped away.*]

Look at Mrs Murry! This proves it. Mrs Murry should be in a sanatorium.

GURDJIEFF: If someone asks for help I must give.

ASANOV: It is not helping if she dies. People will say you killed her.

GURDJIEFF: You go now, Asanov. Dig!

ASANOV: And then what happens? There go your rich Americans! Haida! Top speed! No more Institute for the Harmonious Development of Man.

[*He exits. A pause.*]

GURDJIEFF: There is much suffering in the world. Hardest part of my work is when see and cannot help. Worse because this suffering serve no useful purpose, because people do not know how to use.

[*Pause.*]

That is my suffering: that they do not know.

[*He looks at* VERA.]

Vera. Midnight. After Study House. You come to my room.

[*They exit in opposite directions.*]

SCENE THREE

Fontainebleau, 1922: The gallery above the cowshed. LIDIA
joins KATHERINE. *She carries two candles.*

LIDIA: It's getting dark.
   [*She sets the candles on the floor and kneels to light them.*]
   Katherine?
KATHERINE: I'm alright, Lidia.
LIDIA: Does it hurt?
KATHERINE: My right lung. But then it always does more or
   less. It helps if I do this.
   [*She raises her right arm in a gesture like the first se-
   quence from the dance, then smiles.*]
   But it's hardly a permanent solution.
   [*She lowers her arm. They sit in silence.* KATHERINE
   draws strength from LIDIA'S *presence.*]
LIDIA: Do you regret coming to Fontainebleau?
KATHERINE: No. This place proves how wrong the doctors
   were. I would have been dead fifty times if I'd listened to
   them. [*With affection*] I used to think, if there was one thing
   I couldn't bear in a community, it would be the women. But,
   Lidia, the women are nearer and far dearer to me than the
   men.
   [LIDIA *takes her hand*]
   I was afraid coming here. So many voices said, 'Don't do
   it'...But someone had to help me.
   [*Pause.*]
   In the past all my biggest mistakes were because I was afraid
   and didn't face things. It's taken me till now to understand
   this. If we set out on a journey we must submit to the jour-
   ney. We're afraid. We resist. The little boat enters the dark
   gulf and our only wish is to escape: 'Put me on land again'
   But it's no use. The shadowy figure rows on. One ought to
   sit still and uncover one's eyes.
LIDIA: What do you think you will see, Katherine?
KATHERINE: The truth.

LIDIA: Perhaps we're not meant to see. The shadowy figure says remove the mask but not the blindfold. Perhaps he doesn't want you to see.

KATHERINE: But this is what we're here for, isn't it?

LIDIA: Some of us followed Gurdjieff because we knew he could get us safely out of Russia. Not because we were disciples.

KATHERINE: But you chose to follow.

LIDIA: We chose to live. We walked, for two months, across the mountains to the Black Sea. Whenever we came to Bolshevik or White Army lines Gurdjieff would go forward and say that we were an archaeological expedition. Then he would turn and rub his moustache, either the right side or the left, telling us which set of papers to produce.

KATHERINE: You put your trust in him utterly.

LIDIA: Many times. If he had made a mistake we would have been shot.

KATHERINE: And now?

LIDIA: I work hard. I earn my keep. But it isn't home.

KATHERINE: Yet you stay.

LIDIA: My family died in the massacre at Pyatigorsk. I have one photograph to say they ever existed.

KATHERINE: And yourself.

LIDIA: And myself.

KATHERINE: You have so much life ahead of you, Lidia. Don't you see a future beyond here?

[LIDIA *is silent.*]

You mean Gurdjieff has put himself in place of your family?

LIDIA: Gurdjieff has put himself in place of my soul.

[*Pause.*]

He says that for women there must be two people; that for a woman to progress in the Work she must have a man beside her. There are more women here than men, so usually he is the man.

[*As* KATHERINE *stares at* LIDIA, VERA *and* ASANOV *enter. They pick up* KATHERINE's *trunk and start to exit with it.*]

KATHERINE: What are you doing?

ASANOV: Mr Gurdjieff says you're leaving.

[KATHERINE *is shocked.*]

VERA: Take no notice of him. Asanov just means the Master
   is putting you in the Ritz.

KATHERINE: Why?

LIDIA: It's the warmest room in the house.

ASANOV: Just be grateful you're not in the Monk's Corridor
   with us.

KATHERINE: But I like this place. I've grown attached to it.

ASANOV: That's why you're being moved.

   [VERA *and* ASANOV *continue with the trunk.*]

KATHERINE: I don't suppose you've seen my laundry?

ASANOV: Your laundry is gone.

KATHERINE: Yes, I know it's gone. I sent it days ago.

ASANOV: Stolen.

KATHERINE: What?

VERA: The laundry people are still looking, but we're afraid
   there has been a thief.

LIDIA: You haven't lost everything?

KATHERINE: Two week's worth. Every shred.

ASANOV: It is a shock for you, Katherine.

   [*He smiles.*]

But shocks are important in the Work. They keep us awake!

   [*He exits with* VERA. *Lights fade on* KATHERINE *and* LIDIA.
   They exit.]

SCENE FOUR

The ward. The MAN *is at the window in his wheelchair. He stares
out, his body motionless, his gaze fixed.* WAYNE *comes in. He
has a book balanced on his head. He pauses, staring at the*
MAN's *back, then walks across to him, the book still balanced
on his head, as if practising deportment.*

WAYNE: Lovely day.

   [*The* MAN *ignores him.*]

Did you eat your breakfast?

   [*Pause.*]

I can find out. Whatever's wrong with you, you won't help
it by not eating.

[*Pause.*]

You've got to stop moping. 'A man's reach should exceed
his grasp', remember?

MAN: 'Or what's a heaven for?'

WAYNE: Eh?

[*The book falls unheeded. He reaches for a pencil and
paper and writes.*]

'A man's reach should exceed his grasp or what's a heaven
for?' [*He takes it in.*] Shit!

MAN: [*staring at the book*] What's that?

WAYNE: It's a book.

MAN: [*with an edge*] I can see it's a book. What is it?

WAYNE: This? Oh, it's nothing much: 'The Collected Stories
of Katherine Mansfield'

MAN: Give it to me!

[*The MAN grabs it.*]

MAN: Can there be so much?

[*He opens it to the contents page. He smiles.*] 'Prelude'
...'Bliss'...'The Garden Party'...

[*He frowns.*]

'Unfinished Stories'? 'Father and the Girls' 'Second Violin'
'The Dove's Nest'...But those weren't ready...

[*Pause.*]

God's! He's published everything!

WAYNE: He?

MAN: Jack!

WAYNE: That's nothing. There's 'The Journal of Katherine
Mansfield', 'The scrapbook of Katherine Mansfield', 'The
Unpublished Manuscripts of Katherine Mansfield' -

[*The MAN rises from the chair.*]

MAN: I said leave all fair!

[*He swings his stick in a wide arc and smashes the window. WAYNE leaps back.*]

WAYNE: What the fuck -

MAN: [*slashing at the glass*] Tear up and burn! Publish as
little as possible!

WAYNE: Are you crazy?

[*He tries to take the stick. The* MAN *raises it threatening-ly*.]

MAN: Leave me!

WAYNE: You bloody lunatic! Look what you've done!

MAN: What *I've* done? What about *him*?

[*Another swipe at the glass.*]

WAYNE: How the fuck am I going to explain a broken window? That's my job, mate. My fucking job!

MAN: Don't you swear at me.

WAYNE: [*incredulous*] What?

[*Pause.*]

Listen. You'd better wake up to a few things around here. So far I've protected you. Stopped too many questions being asked. What do I say now? You go berko and I'm responsible. I should just leave you to it.

MAN: Leave!

WAYNE: Thanks. Terrific.

[*He moves to go.*]

MAN: He turned me into an industry.

WAYNE: Yeah? [*Maliciously*] He had a farm to run. Wives to support.

MAN: Wives?

WAYNE: Four of them. He married the second one because she reminded him of Katherine. She even managed to die of T.B. The next one used to beat him up. Bit of a masochist if you ask me. Seems to have been happy with the last one though.

MAN: You're making this up, Asanov.

WAYNE: You want to get to the library, mate. Read your own biographies - or whoever the hell's they are.

[WAYNE *turns to leave.*]

MAN: Wait. I know what you're doing, Asanov.

[*He gets back in the wheel-chair.* WAYNE *stops.*]

I know you're paid to stay here -

WAYNE: [*interrupting*] Yeah, I'm paid. And it's going to take me a year to cover that window!

MAN: He pays you to stay so you can torment us - not just me but everyone at the Institute.

WAYNE: What are you talking about?

MAN: Sometimes you even have me believing your stories, even though I know the reason for them.

WAYNE: What reason?

MAN: He knows you annoy us and that's how he makes us aware of our negative emotions.

WAYNE: Thanks very much. Will he pay for the window as well?

MAN: No, no. I'll pay for it. It's part of my lesson. Next time I'll try not to let you provoke me.

WAYNE: Wonderful.

[*He turns to go.*]

MAN: Asanov -

WAYNE: My name isn't Asanov!

MAN: May we call a truce?

WAYNE: A truce.

MAN: I know I'm not supposed to read books or write letters, but could you get me some?

WAYNE: What?

MAN: Books!

WAYNE: Why should I do anything for you?

MAN: Because I crave them. Some Shakespeare -

WAYNE: Who?

MAN: Shakespeare. 'But I tell you, my Lord fool, Out of this nettle danger, we pluck this flower, safety'...Yes. Get me that...And some Chekhov!...Thomas Hardy!...Even Lawrence. Yes. No matter how much one may disagree. Even what one objects to is a sign of life in him. He's a living man! When he mentions gooseberries these are real, red, ripe gooseberries that the gardener is rolling on a tray. When he bites into an apple it is a sharp, sweet, fresh apple from the growing tree -

WAYNE: Gooseberries, eh? Apples. What about a truckload of pineapples from north Queensland? Or some oranges from the Murrumbidgee?

MAN: [*indicating the* Collected Stories] If you can get me this you can get me some Shakespeare.

WAYNE: I can get myself arrested. There are no books by men. None. They still exist but they're not available to us. [*Indicating the* Stories] I can borrow something like that because it's written by a ...It's written by a woman!

[*The* MAN *opens the book.*]

MAN: Dear boy, tell the Master you've been a good chap and
  done your job, but now I need to rest and think...perhaps
  even write something.

WAYNE: What's the point? It'll never be published! [*In pity*]
  Okay. Sure. Everyone should have a hobby. I do a bit of
  scribbling myself.

  [*The* MAN'*s gaze is cold.*]

MAN: When I write a story I choose not only the length of every
  sentence, but the sound. I choose the rise and fall of every
  paragraph to fit the mood or the character on *that* day at that
  moment. After I've written it I read it aloud, until I get it
  right, until there's not a single word out of place, and not
  one word that could be taken out. While I am writing I am
  engulfed. Possessed. Anyone who comes near is my enemy.
  It takes the place of religion for me. It *is* my religion. Get
  me a tuppeny notebook and a pen that won't leak. Tell the
  Master if you must, but get them.

WAYNE: There's no point in writing if you feel like that about
  it. It just makes it worse. I mean look at you: you know all
  this stuff and you don't feel any better than I do.

MAN: I don't want to die with my work unfinished!

WAYNE: You're not dying!

MAN: I feel nauseated all the time. There's a kind of boom-
  ing in my head. I haven't done the work I should have done.

WAYNE: I'll get you a biro. Okay?

MAN: I shall need a table, a pot of yellow paint and a brush if
  you can manage it, a straight-backed chair that doesn't wob-
  ble - an office chair would be even better - flowers and a
  vase -

WAYNE: Anything else?

MAN: I tend to be something of a clock-watcher. I like to know
  when dinner-time's near.

WAYNE: Anything in particular you'd like to eat?

MAN: Just get me a notebook and a pen. Even though I know
  you're doing it against the Master's wishes, it's still a kindness to me.

WAYNE: A kindness.

  [*Pause.*]

You poor bastard. You poor bloody fool...I thought I knew about hopeless.

> [*He goes out. Lights fade. The* MAN *exits, the wheelchair remains.*]

SCENE FIVE

Fontainebleau, 1922. The Ritz. KATHERINE *looks critically at her new quarters.* GURDJIEFF *watches her and smokes, an echo of their first scene.*

KATHERINE: Isaiah - or was it Elisha? - was caught up into heaven in a chariot of fire *once*. But when I'm writing, a journey like that is positively nothing. I don't care for the Ritz. It reminds me of Garsington.

GURDJIEFF: Garsington?

KATHERINE: A country house in England presided over by a literary patroness, Lady Ottoline. Crammed every weekend with intellectuals. The house, not Ottoline - though that equally could be said. There. I'm even talking that way again.

GURDJIEFF: Good for you.

KATHERINE: Good? What's good about it?

GURDJIEFF: Can see that you have changed.

KATHERINE: Passed another lampost, have I? Yes! I've done it. Put off the old and put on the new. That's why I must start writing again - because what I have to say now is new for me. No more stories like little birds bred in cages. I want to write in a way that's hopeful, not satirical or disillusioned. And I can do that better where I was.

GURDJIEFF: Is better you are here.

KATHERINE: Better for whom? I wasn't particularly disturbing the cows. They quite liked me. And I've certainly grown to like them. I'd hoped to stay in my old place until I leave.

GURDJIEFF: You will leave from this room.

KATHERINE: I may sound pernickety, but one of the worst things about France is there's never anywhere comfortable to sit.

GURDJIEFF: I will have divan brought from other room.

KATHERINE: You're very careful of me suddenly. Why not bring *me* to the divan?

GURDJIEFF: Is better you have company.

KATHERINE: I had excellent company. Equivoquetecka, Bridget, Mitasha and Baldaofim. And when Bridget had her calf I watched while Lidia and Madame Ostrovsky tied a rope around its leg and pulled it out.

   [*She falls silent.*]

I'm not stupid. Normally you'd have the entire household in transit.

GURDJIEFF: Doctor Resnais.

KATHERINE: Oh.

   [*Pause.*]

Where?

GURDJIEFF: He will hear if you ring.

KATHERINE: This really is the Ritz. Send up a doctor, please, I'm dying.

   [*Pause.*]

I wanted the truth, didn't I? I expect he can do more for me than Bridget, though not much.

   [*She moves away to the opposite side of the stage, her back to him.*]

I'd like to see Jack.

GURDJIEFF: He will be honoured guest.

KATHERINE: When?

GURDJIEFF: After New Year.

KATHERINE: That's in - that's very soon.

   [*She turns.*]

What did she mean? Lidia. 'For women there must be two people'?

   [*As the lights change* KATHERINE *and* GURDJIEFF *could remain where they are.*]

SCENE SIX

The ward. AUDRA *enters. The wheelchair is near the broken window. It is unoccupied.*

AUDRA: [*with false cheer*] Well, how are we today? Who are
    we today?
       [*She sees the empty chair. Her voice hardens.*]
    Where are we today?
       [*She goes over to the window.*]
    Congratulations. A sense of logic at last.
       [*She looks down at the street.*]
    Odd...
       [*She gives a little shrug then sits in the wheelchair and
       propels herself about for a turn or two.* WAYNE *comes
       in carrying a bucket and a notebook and pen.*]
    Push me.
       [WAYNE *stares from* AUDRA *to the window. She wheels
       away from him. Her back is to him.*]
WAYNE: What?
AUDRA: Push me!
       [WAYNE *ignores her.*]
WAYNE: Where is he?
       [*She turns.*]
AUDRA: Where is who?
WAYNE: The man!
AUDRA: There's no one here but me. I'm no man.
WAYNE: What have you done with him?
AUDRA: [*indicating the window*] If you had anything to do
    with that you'll have to pay for it.
WAYNE: I don't care about the bloody window! Where is he?
AUDRA: You *should* care.
WAYNE: Where is he?
AUDRA: Gone.
       [WAYNE *looks down from the window.*]
    You see? Nothing. Up in smoke. Vanished. Good rid-
    dance.

WAYNE: You unfeeling bitch! I'll bloody push you alright!

AUDRA: Watch it. I suspect you're in enough trouble already.

WAYNE: Then a bit more won't matter!

[*He grasps the wheelchair and propels it towards the window*.]

AUDRA: [*alarmed*] What are you doing?

WAYNE: You wanted a push, didn't you?

[*He grabs her hair as she tries to rise.*]

AUDRA: Let go.

[*He brings the chair to a halt in front of the opening.*]

WAYNE: Now -

AUDRA: Let go of me!

WAYNE: A few questions.

AUDRA: Let go!

WAYNE: Did you buy a paper this morning?

AUDRA: No!

WAYNE: Did you buy a paper yesterday?

[*He wrenches her head back*]

AUDRA: No. I didn't buy a paper yesterday.

WAYNE: Why not?

AUDRA: You're going to be sorry!

WAYNE: So are you. Yesterday!

AUDRA: What about it?

WAYNE: And the day before. And the day before that. You don't buy papers.

AUDRA: No.

WAYNE: I do.

AUDRA: You're insane and I'll see you're dealt with.

WAYNE: I buy a paper every day to find out what poor bastard jumped last night. Drowned himself. O.D.'d. It's time you learned how the other half dies, Audra.

AUDRA: [*genuinely alarmed now*] Let me go.

WAYNE: I can't, you stupid bitch.

AUDRA: I won't turn round. I won't Look at you. Not after what we've been.

WAYNE: [*yanking her head back*] What have we been?

[AUDRA *moans.*]

Are you in pain?

AUDRA: Yes!

WAYNE: Good. Because it's nothing to what I feel. You've killed the only human being that ever meant a fucking thing to me.

AUDRA: I didn't touch him, I swear!

WAYNE: The only thing that ever made any *sense*!

AUDRA: What sense? You don't even know who he was!

WAYNE: And now I'll never know - thanks to you.

AUDRA: Why don't you ask Rahel?

WAYNE: Rahel?

AUDRA: He was her patient. She'll tell you.

WAYNE: She didn't know who he was.

AUDRA: She knows! Ask her! Ask Rahel!

>   [WAYNE *steps back*. AUDRA *feels the release. She gets up*. WAYNE *grabs her hair and yanks her down again. He grabs the bucket and inverts it over her head. He spins the chair and pushes it off stage*.]

WAYNE: Tell me about *Heaven*, Audra!

>   [*He runs for the opposite exit*.]

SCENE SEVEN

Fontainebleau, 1922. The Ritz. KATHERINE *and* GURDJIEFF *continue from Scene Five*.

KATHERINE: Tell me what she meant - Lidia. She said you had put yourself in place of her soul.

GURDJIEFF: Necessary.

KATHERINE: Why?

GURDJIEFF: Woman is from ground. Self development not possible for her unless she is with man.

KATHERINE: Good God...

GURDJIEFF: You know that here we do not speak of God. This beyond pupils' understanding.

KATHERINE: I wonder what I *have* understood.

GURDJIEFF: Only way for woman to evolve - go to what you call 'Heaven'- is with man.

KATHERINE: If one happens to have misplaced one's man?

GURDJIEFF: She does not go anywhere.

KATHERINE: We don't cross the border without you? You provide the passport? Password? Maps?

GURDJIEFF: Good. Understand now.

KATHERINE: What do I understand?

GURDJIEFF: This why you are here.

KATHERINE: I'm here because I thought a sanatorium would be a second lunatic asylum!

GURDJIEFF: It is not wise to tell pupils all the truth at once.

KATHERINE: Certainly not. There'd be nobody in the Monks' Corridor. People don't like being told which end of the pigsty they should occupy. Particularly if its the wrong end.

GURDJIEFF: I can not help someone who does not face the truth.

KATHERINE: Oh, yes. Truth. Why don't I recognise it by now? 'Get well? Of course you will! We'll put you right in no time!' You're no better than Manoukhin.

GURDJIEFF: I am not doctor. Not promise cure.

KATHERINE: No. I wanted you to cure my soul.

GURDJIEFF: You do not have a soul.

KATHERINE: What about you? If you've got one and I haven't, it's not hard to guess where you keep it. May I have a cigarette?

GURDJIEFF: You should not smoke.

> [KATHERINE *smiles. He gives her a cigarette and lights it for her.*]

KATHERINE: If heaven's no place for a woman on her own I think I'm better off.

GURDJIEFF: This earth very bad place.

KATHERINE: Not for me.

GURDJIEFF: Very little is possible for woman. On earth is man, not woman, who climb mountains, paint picture, write books-

> [KATHERINE *picks up a copy of her stories,* 'Bliss', *and holds it aloft.*]

There are women try to become man, but this wrong for her nature. Man has aspiration to find heaven because has possibility for immortality. But such aspiration poison for woman unless has man to help her.

KATHERINE: The way you helped Lidia?

> [*Pause.*]

And all those other women you refer to as your 'cows', with their 'calves', who look so remarkably like you. Why isn't it in your prospectus? 'Women will be assisted from this world by the Master, G.I.Gurdjieff, providing they become cattle to his bidding'.

GURDJIEFF: Without me never be anything *but* cow. When die only have value for fertiliser.

KATHERINE: I could get on a train to Paris. Though what would be the point? I've scarcely a petticoat to fly with in any case. You don't own a factory that makes ladies' underwear by any chance? No. You can supply me with false eyelashes, can't you? Or a Persian carpet. Can you send me off on one of those?

[*Lights fade.* GURDJIEFF *exits.*]

SCENE EIGHT

The MAN *lies face down at the foot of the wall bearing the words 'MY LORD FOOL', with the* 'Collected Stories', *pages loose and scattered, lying on the ground nearby.* WAYNE *enters. He picks up the pages nearest him, registers what they are, then sees the* MAN. *He approaches slowly, crouches and feels the* MAN's *pulse. Very carefully he turns him over. Lights change.* WAYNE *cradles the* MAN *in his arms.*

KATHERINE: I must tell you a dream. The first night I was here I went to sleep. And suddenly I felt my whole body breaking up. It broke with a violent shock - an earthquake - and it broke like glass. A long terrible shiver, and the spinal cord and the bones and every bit and particle quaking. It sounded in my ears: a low, confused din, and there was a sense of flashing greenish brilliance, like broken glass. When I woke up I thought there had been a violent earthquake. But all was still. It slowly dawned upon me that in that dream I died. I was no longer afraid. The spirit that is the enemy of death and quakes so and is so tenacious of life was shaken out of me. Time is not. I am, January the ninth, 1923, a dead woman.

[*The* MAN *begins to cough.*]

WAYNE: [*with relief*] You stupid bastard! You just walk out? You don't say anything? And look at this - that's a library book!

[*He starts to lift the* MAN. *The* MAN's *breathing is laboured. He puts a hand to his chest in pain.* RAHEL *enters.*]

RAHEL: Leave him!

WAYNE: I thought he was dead.

RAHEL: He is. As good as.

MAN: [*slurred*] Get well? Of course you will...

WAYNE: Audra says there's nothing wrong with him!

RAHEL: [*quietly*] He's dying all the same.

[WAYNE *stares at her.*]

I made him. Or what you think is him. You can give anybody a history that never happened and they'll believe it.

WAYNE: That's crazy.

RAHEL: I created a man who could be an equal, without being a danger - that's not crazy.

WAYNE: But you made him believe he was someone who was going to die!

RAHEL: I gave him her thoughts and feelings, not her physical decay. But when he woke up, he knew more than I'd given him. He knew things I hadn't told him.

WAYNE: Look at him. He can't breathe! Can't you help him?

RAHEL: I can make him what he was.

WAYNE: Then do it!

RAHEL: Is that what you want?

[WAYNE *watches as the* MAN *struggles for breath.*]

WAYNE: [*slowly*] There'll be no Katherine Mansfield...

RAHEL: No.

WAYNE: No Keats...or Shelley.

[*Pause.*]

What will he be?

[*Pause.*]

RAHEL: [*simply*] He'll be alive...like you.

[WAYNE *is silent. He looks up at the wall.*]

WAYNE: [*to himself*] 'My lord fool...'

RAHEL: [*quietly*] What do you want me to do?

[WAYNE *turns away.*]

WAYNE: Kill him.

[*He walks away.* RAHEL *stands a moment, then exits.
Lights up on* KATHERINE.]

KATHERINE: Shall I be able to express, one day, my love of
work - my desire to be a better writer - my longing to take
greater pains. And the passion I feel. It takes the place of
religion - it is my religion.

Oh, God! The sky is filled with the sun, and the sun is like
music. The sky is full of music. Music comes streaming
down these great beams. The wind touches the trees, shakes
little jets of music. The shape of every flower is like a
sound. My hands open like five petals.

Isaiah - or was it Elisha? - was caught up into Heaven in a
chariot of fire *once*. But when the weather is divine and I
am free to work, such a journey is positively nothing...
Cold. Still. The gale last night has blown nearly all the
snow off the trees; only big, frozen-looking lumps remain.
In the wood where the snow is thick, bars of sunlight lay
like pale fire.

I want to remember how the light fades from a room - and
one fades with it, is expunged, sitting still, knees together,
hands in pockets...

I would like to hear Jack saying 'We'll have the north
meadow mowed tomorrow', on a late evening in summer,
when our shadows were like a pair of scissors, and we could
just see the rabbits in the dark.

[*The lights fade.*]

THE END

Also available from Currency Press

BLOOD RELATIONS - David Malouf
In this his first play, the award-winning novelist peoples his stage with characters whose inner selves are as immediate as their environment. A family group gathers at Christmas about the dynamic and manipulative patriarch, Willy - a man with many pasts. They are joined by two inquisitive characters bent on uncovering his secret. The revelation uncovers a further mystery of guilt and reconciliation.

ESSINGTON LEWIS: I AM WORK - John O'Donoghue
Based on the life of Essington Lewis, the industrialist who was the driving force behind the growth of BHP, the plays uses music and lyrics by Allen McFadden to enhance the portrait of this very powerful character.

EUROPE and ON TOP OF THE WORLD - Michael Gow
Two fine plays from the author of *Away*. In *Europe* a young Australian travels in pursuit of an actress with whom he has had a brief affair. The sudden encounter of the old world by the new triggers an emotional series of revelations. *On Top of the World* takes a different perspective on history. In a Gold Coast apartment a family ritual assumes awesome proportions as the dying generation and its lost children together discover a resilient new humanity.

CONTEMPORARY AUSTRALIAN DRAMA - Edited by Peter Holloway. Second Edition.
A collection of articles by critics such as Clive James, Katharine Brisbane, Leonard Radic, H.G. Kippax, Brian Kernan, Margaret Williams and many more, offering the best in literary criticism of our living drama. In addition to the best of the first edition, this volume adds major new writing on Ray Mathew, David Williamson, Dorothy Hewett, Patrick White, John Romeril, Alexander Buzo, Stephen Sewell and Louis Nowra amongst others. Added for the first time as a vital reference is a biographical checklist of seventy playwrights now working in the Australian theatre.

Contact Currency Press, P.O. Box 452, Paddington, NSW 2021 for more information.